D0938915

A BLUE BANNER BIOGRAPHY

Alan Jackson

Jennifer Torres

Mitchell Lane
PUBLISHERS

P.O. Box 196
Hockessin, Delaware 19707
Visit us on the web: www.mitchelllane.com
Comments? email us: mitchelllane@mitchelllane.com

JB
JACKSON

Printing   1   2   3   4   5   6   7   8   9

Blue Banner Biographies

Alan Jackson	Alicia Keys	Allen Iverson
Ashanti	Ashlee Simpson	Ashton Kutcher
Avril Lavigne	Bernie Mac	Beyoncé
Bow Wow	Britney Spears	Christina Aguilera
Christopher Paul Curtis	Clay Aiken	Condoleezza Rice
Daniel Radcliffe	Derek Jeter	Eminem
Eve	50 Cent	Gwen Stefani
Ice Cube	Jamie Foxx	Ja Rule
Jay-Z	Jennifer Lopez	J. K. Rowling
Jodie Foster	Justin Berfield	Kate Hudson
Kelly Clarkson	Kenny Chesney	Lance Armstrong
Lindsay Lohan	Mariah Carey	Mario
Mary-Kate and Ashley Olsen	Melissa Gilbert	Michael Jackson
Miguel Tejada	Missy Elliott	Nelly
Orlando Bloom	P. Diddy	Paris Hilton
Peyton Manning	Queen Latifah	Rita Williams-Garcia
Ritchie Valens	Ron Howard	Rudy Giuliani
Sally Field	Selena	Shirley Temple
Tim McGraw	Usher	

Library of Congress Cataloging-in-Publication Data
Torres, Jennifer.
Alan Jackson/Jennifer Torres.   W A
        p. cm. — (Blue banner biographies)
   Includes bibliographical references, discography (p.), and index.
   ISBN 1-58415-504-3 (library bound)
      1. Jackson, Alan, 1958—Juvenile literature. 2. Country musicians—United States—
Biography—Juvenile literature. I. Title. II. Blue banner biography.
   ML3930.J145T67 2007
   782.421642092—dc22
                                                                       2006006094
ISBN–10: 1-58415-504-3   ISBN–13: 978-158415-504-1

ABOUT THE AUTHOR: Jennifer Torres is a freelance writer and newspaper columnist based in Central Florida. Her articles have appeared in newspapers, parenting journals, and women's magazines across the country and Canada. When she's not writing she enjoys spending time at the beach with her husband John and their five children, Timothy, Emily, Isabelle, Daniel, and Jacqueline.

PHOTO CREDITS: cover, p. 4—AdMedia/WireImage.com; p. 7—Alan L. Mayor/WireImage.com; p. 9—Larry Busacca/WireImage.com; p. 12—Frank Micellotta/ImageDirect; p. 16—Time Life Pictures/DMI/Getty Images; p. 19—James Schnepf/Getty Images; p. 21—Scott Gries/Getty Images; p. 24—Michael Caulfield/WireImage.com; p. 26—Scott Gries/Getty Images; p. 28 Ben Rose/WireImage.com

CONTENTS

Alan Jackson at the 2002 American Society of Composers, Authors and Publishers (ASCAP) Country Music Awards in Nashville, Tennessee. At the ceremony, ASCAP honored him with a career achievement Golden Note Award and a Songwriter/Artist of the Year award.

CHAPTER 1

"Where Were You When the World Stopped Turning?"

With an eight-word question, country singing superstar Alan Jackson helped heal a nation that was terribly wounded and looking for hope. The song, written just weeks after fanatical terrorists killed more than 3,000 innocent people in several American cities, seemed to come at just the right moment with the perfect tone.

The ballad was not filled with anger or rage. It did not talk of revenge or striking back or going to war. It simply asked people if they remembered where they were when they first heard of the terrorist attacks of September 11, 2001, known now as 9/11.

Then somehow, using the simplest of melodies and very limited instruments, the song was able to remind listeners of the important things in life. Jackson, singing in a voice that seemed to be near tears, tells listeners about the beauty of sunsets, making friends with strangers, taking that old Bible off a shelf and actually reading it, or just calling your mother to let her know you love her.

Then during the sing-along chorus, Jackson tells listeners where his inspiration truly comes from. He recalls a childhood lesson he learned in Sunday school recognizing faith, hope, and love as the three most valuable gifts God has given to man, with the greatest being love.

Maybe this was how angry Americans would have to get through the worst terrorist attack ever on American soil. Maybe this was how they were supposed to move on even as the memories of lost loved ones haunted their dreams. Maybe all they had to do was remember God and the gift of love.

The first time Jackson played the song live was on national television at the 2001 Country Music Association Awards. There was not a dry eye in the house. The switchboards lit up at radio and television stations across the country. People wanted to know what the song was called and where they could get it.

Jackson, like most Americans, had been haunted by those terrible images of the terrorist attacks. He admired the firefighters and police officers who bravely entered the World Trade Center looking for survivors. He watched the tapes and the news shows with his wife and cried. One night, while trying to escape the images and get some sleep, a line entered his head: "Where were you when the world stopped turning?" He got up and sang the first few lines into a tape recorder.

> *Jackson, like most Americans, had been haunted by those terrible images of the terrorist attacks.*

Jackson performs at the 2001 Country Music Association Awards, where he debuted his patriotic hit "Where Were You When the World Stopped Turning?"

The next morning, Jackson wrote the entire song, though he won't take credit for it.

"God wrote it," he said. "I just held the pencil."

Jackson discovered while he was writing one of the greatest country songs ever that he had been feeling guilty.

He felt guilty that so many firefighters and other heroes died, and here he was singing songs.

"What am I doing here, just writing and singing songs?" he asked himself. "I was thinking what I did for a living wasn't worth a whole lot."

He was wrong.

His song helped a nation when it was down. And it wasn't just country fans who loved the song. It appealed to millions who had feelings of guilt or sadness because of what happened.

The song was something that Jackson felt he had to write and sing. He felt it would help him deal with his own feelings. Never did he imagine how much of a hit it would become and what it would do for his career.

When the inspiring anthem hit the airwaves, this song catapulted him into legendary status.

Although Jackson was already a country music superstar when the inspiring anthem hit the airwaves, this song catapulted him into legendary status. Just a year after the song brought the nation together, he took home a record-tying five major awards at the 36th Annual Country Music Association Awards (CMA). The CMAs are the most prestigious awards for all of country music. Winning a CMA means you've been accepted by your fans, your peers, and the music industry as a whole.

A humble and sometimes painfully shy Jackson walked to the podium and accepted the Entertainer of the Year

Signing autographs during a perfomance in New York City, Jackson mingles with his fans.

award, as well as prizes for Single of the Year and Song of the Year. He also was named Male Vocalist of the Year, and his *Drive* won Album of the Year.

Jackson had surely come a long way from the Georgia country boy whose first job wasn't even in music. No, when Alan was twelve, he worked in a shoe repair shop for a cobbler.

Growing Up Country

Alan Eugene Jackson was born on October 17, 1958, in the small town of Newnan, Georgia. The population of Newnan is only 15,000, and it sits just west of the middle part of the state.

His was a typical southern blue-collar family. Alan's father worked as an auto mechanic and made just enough money to support his family of seven. One year, when his parents couldn't really afford to buy Christmas presents for their five children, Alan's father built his son a red go-kart. He still calls that present the best toy he ever got.

You see, Alan's mother had taught him and his four sisters a good sense of values and integrity. It wasn't the monetary value of things that was important to the family, but instead the meaning and the love behind any gift.

As a child Alan enjoyed singing—as many children do—and learned a lot by singing gospel music in church on Sundays. When he wasn't in church there was one place where anybody looking could catch up with him: the local fishing hole. Alan loved — and still loves — spending his day by throwing a worm into the pond and fishing. As a child, he would fish alone or with his dad. Sometimes he would go with his best childhood friend — his pet, a spider monkey named Peanuts.

When Alan got just a little bit older he discovered the classic country music of legendary singer Hank Williams. What Alan liked so much about the music was the raw, real sound. He also loved how he could identify with the lyrics and with how much he felt he had in common with Williams.

"I always felt this connection with Hank," Jackson said. "The way he grew up reminded me of my life, with Baptist hymns and dirt in your yard instead of grass. I always felt I grew up under similar conditions, with the whole rural Southern kind of family, but I had a lot nicer life."

In a family of seven, if you wanted spending money, you had better find yourself a job. When Alan turned twelve he started working for a shoe repair shop. This would start a long stretch of odd jobs that Alan would have until he made it big in Nashville as a country singer.

Maybe it was because the family did not have a lot of money to buy fancy clothes, or maybe it was just the fact that the tall, skinny kid idolized the simple-living Hank Williams — whatever the reason, Alan shirked the fancy

> *When Alan got just a little bit older he discovered the classic country music of legendary singer Hank Williams.*

Alan and Denise Jackson walk the red carpet at the Country Music Association Awards in 2000. Thanks in part to his wife's support and daring, Alan Jackson has become a famous country music star.

clothes that some of his friends were wearing and always wore a tee-shirt and blue jeans.

There probably is no reason behind his favorite snack as a kid and his favorite sandwich as a grown-up: a pineapple and mayonnaise sandwich! Wow, now that's different.

He went to Newnan High School, where many kids were really getting into music. Alan already knew the words to all of Hank Williams' songs, but he was also into the rebellious country songs of Merle Haggard — and now he wanted a guitar. Knowing his parents did not have a lot of money, he was afraid to ask for one. Finally he got up the courage to ask and they agreed. He was sixteen years old, and this request would change his life — though he wouldn't know it for many years. They bought a used guitar for $50, an investment of a lifetime.

Alan basically taught himself how to play and soon enough he found himself in a high school band named Dixie Steel — the same name of a brand of construction nails used in the South. The group soon dwindled to a duo, but it was a great place for Alan to hone his songwriting skills. The group enjoyed the usual success of high school bands — some kids liked them and some kids hated them.

> *Alan taught himself how to play the guitar and soon enough he found himself in a high school band named Dixie Steel.*

One kid who didn't hate them was a girl named Denise. Alan met Denise while he was buying ice cream at the Newnan Dairy Queen. She was pretty and had a nice personality. The two of them hit it off immediately. Alan asked her if she would like to go on a date. That was the last girlfriend he would ever have. Denise would later become his wife as Alan Jackson, just like in one of his country songs, married his high school sweetheart.

Marrying Denise in a few years would not only be great for Alan's spirit, it would also be great for his career.

CHAPTER 3

On His Way

*F*or the Jacksons, married life was wonderful. Alan and Denise may not have had a lot of money, but the one thing they did have was a lot of love.

To support himself and his new wife, Jackson worked hard. First he was a car salesman, then a construction worker, and then a forklift operator at Kmart.

He also loved to play hard, spending much of his free time with Denise and other friends fishing and listening to music. His favorite artists still included Hank Williams Sr. and Merle Haggard. He also kept his dream of being a country songwriter alive by continuing to write and perform with Dixie Steel.

Denise had a dream, too. She wanted to travel. Becoming a flight attendant seemed like the perfect job. Flight attendants work aboard airplanes as they travels to various cities around the world, serving passengers and helping teach air safety.

There was only one problem, and it was a big one: The newlyweds would have to live apart for six months while she trained for her new job. Alan knew the career move was important to his wife, and he supported her fully. The couple talked on the phone a lot during her training.

Being alone did have one good side: It gave Alan time to really focus on his songwriting. He wrote day and night. Many of his songs were based on the love he felt for his wife.

After becoming a full-fledged flight attendant, Denise returned home to her husband. She began working a normal schedule that took her out of town two or three days a week, leaving the rest of the week for her to be with Alan.

One day, while waiting to board a flight, Denise spotted someone who looked very familiar. At first she thought it couldn't be, but it was!

The man who looked familiar was country superstar Glen Campbell.

> *One day, while waiting to board a flight, Denise spotted country superstar Glen Campbell.*

Campbell was one of the most popular country singers in the 1960s, '70s, and '80s. His hits included "Rhinestone Cowboy," which reached number one on both the country and pop charts. Campbell had also been a touring member of The Beach Boys for a while.

Denise couldn't believe her luck. This was a chance to get her husband's name to someone who could help his music career.

Country powerhouse Garth Brooks (left) and Jackson in 1992. As a struggling musician, Jackson never knew that one day he would be hanging out with country music's stars — and that he would be one himself.

She approached the burly man with a smile, and he greeted her warmly.

Campbell patiently listened as Denise told him all about her talented husband and handed him one of Alan's demo tapes. The tape had a sample of Alan's songs recorded on it. Campbell then gave Denise his business card and told her to have Alan give him a call.

This was beyond exciting! Denise couldn't wait to call her husband and tell him what had just happened.

It probably took a while for Jackson to realize she wasn't kidding. This was the real thing. An opportunity had been handed to him, and he wasn't about to let it pass by.

When Jackson called Campbell's publishing company, Seventh Son, he was encouraged to pursue his dream of a career in music. But, they told him, there was only one place he could really do that: the city of Nashville, Tennessee.

Nashville is known as the capital of country music. Its most popular nickname is Music City USA.

Nashville is known as the capital of country music. Its most popular nickname is Music City USA. The bustling hub is one of the most important music recording cities in the country. The city even has a street called Music Row, where all the big musical artists have recorded their songs, including Faith Hill, Garth Brooks, and the late Elvis Presley.

After a few calls back and forth, the Jacksons were encouraged by Campbell's enthusiasm for Alan's music. In 1985, on his advice, they made the big move to Nashville.

Rise to the Top

As Alan and Denise Jackson adjusted to their new home in Nashville, Alan realized getting noticed in a city of abundant talent wasn't going to be easy. Even with one of country music's biggest celebrities behind him, Alan knew he needed more training. His dream was to be a country songwriter and singer, but it was a dream shared by many other young men and women who also made their home in Nashville. He had to compete with them for what felt like a one-in-a-million chance.

"In retrospect, I realize I was so green," said Jackson. "My writing was green. As a singer, I didn't know what I really needed to sound like. The package wasn't ready yet."

And so, Jackson did what he thought was the next best thing to being a Nashville star: He took a job where he could be close to real Nashville stars, in the mailroom of the Nashville Network.

The downside was he earned only $100 a week. The upside was the fact that down the hall, country favorites like

At home his home at Center Hill Lake, Tennessee, Jackson enjoys the view while strumming his guitar. Jackson named his house Real World, after the title of his first album, Here in the Real World.

Crook & Chase and Ralph Emery produced their popular shows, while country concerts from places like the Grand Ole Opry were beamed into homes across the country from the network's studios.

While there, Jackson made many friends. His easygoing, genuine, down-to-earth nature made him someone people trusted — and noticed.

> His easygoing, genuine, down-to-earth nature made him someone people trusted—and noticed.

He continued to write music and learn from all the mentors who surrounded him. He even got the chance to sing background vocals for a few other country singers.

All of Alan's efforts finally paid off when he was signed on as a staff writer for Seventh Son Music. To keep up his skills as a performer, he played his music after work in as many Nashville clubs as he could.

Writing music was his first love, but being able to sing the words he wrote seemed like the right thing to do. To be noticed as a singer, he'd have to get people to listen to his music. That's where demo tapes come in handy.

The only demo tape he had was the one his wife had handed to Glen Campbell years earlier, and it was in desperate need of an update. He made a new tape with the help of a fellow songwriter named Keith Stegall.

Once again, his efforts paid off. In 1989, Alan Jackson became the very first artist to sign a recording deal with the newest division of the big recording company Arista — its country division.

Alan needed the help of his wife, Denise, and their three daughters — Mattie, 12; Ali, 9; Dani, 5 — to hold all of his trophies at the Annual Country Music Association Awards in 2002.

Country music wasn't just for country music lovers anymore, and record companies were taking note. Companies like Arista, which once signed only pop stars, realized there was a lot of money in country music and wanted a piece of that big country pie.

In 1990, Jackson's first album was released. It was called *Here in the Real World.* The record went gold and then platinum, which means it sold more than 1 million copies. The small-town country boy had made it in the big town of Nashville!

That wasn't the only thing exciting about 1990. On June 19, his first daughter, Mattie Denise, was born. Alan and Denise couldn't have been happier.

Here in the Real World contained four top-five hits, including; "Chasin' That Neon Rainbow," "Wanted," and "I'd Love You All Over Again."

That album was a great accomplishment, but real superstardom came in 1991, with the release of *Don't Rock the Jukebox.* It produced four number-one chart toppers, including the title track, "Someday," "Dallas," and "Love's Got a Hold on You."

One of Alan's own favorite songs was also on the record. It was one he had written about a visit to the grave of Hank Williams, his childhood idol. He called it "Midnight in Montgomery," and it became one of his signature songs, meaning one he is best known for.

Randy Travis asked Alan to help him write several songs on his own album, High Lonesome, and Alan happily agreed.

"Midnight in Montgomery" earned him the Music Video of the Year award from the Country Music Association. He was also nominated for an American Music Award for Favorite New Country Artist.

Jackson's music was making such an impact on country music fans that several country music stars became Alan Jackson fans too. Well-known country crooner Randy Travis was one of them. He asked Jackson to help him write several songs on his own album, *High Lonesome,* and Jackson happily agreed.

Alan and Denise Jackson couldn't believe how far they had come. Within five years of moving to Nashville, Alan had gone from mailroom to mansion. Little did they know, his rise to the top had only just begun.

Country Superstar

*I*n 1993, another blessing came to Alan and Denise when their second daughter, Alexandra Jane, was born on August 23. That same year Alan released a holiday album called *Honky Tonk Christmas.* In what has become Jackson's signature style, he did not use a lot of standard Christmas songs. Instead he preferred to write new music in his own style, which is less glitzy and pop-oriented than that of many of his fellow country singers, such as Garth Brooks and Shania Twain. Jackson likes the old-fashioned type of country music and has been openly disdainful of the pop-music influence that seems to be such a big part of modern country music.

In 1994 he came out with *Who I Am.* Like many of his albums before, it shot straight to number one on the country music charts and produced another four number-one singles. Among them was "Gone Country," in which he makes fun of music executives who don't know anything about country music but suddenly decide to produce it because they want

Jackson presents George Strait with the Gene Weed Special Achievement Award at the Academy of Country Music Awards in 2003. Jackson and Strait collaborated on the song "Murder on Music Row."

to make money. It wouldn't be the last time Jackson took a dig at people he considered phony.

He also joined forces with country singer George Strait for the duet "Murder on Music Row," a salute to traditional country music and a slam at the new wave of country singers whose music sounded too much like pop.

Jackson's story goes on to include a slew of music award nominations and number one albums. His work became recognized and respected worldwide.

Despite all the fame and fortune, family has always been his number one priority.

On Christmas Eve 1996, Alan and Denise gathered their girls around the Christmas tree to make a very special announcement. Denise was pregnant with their third child. Everyone was ecstatic. Dani Grace was born August 28, 1997.

Even with his growing family, Jackson continued to release albums. In 1998 *High Mileage* became his highest-charting album on the pop music charts. Even though being "pop" wasn't ever a goal for Jackson, he was happy his music was being enjoyed by all.

Jackson loves performing, but songwriting is what's closest to his heart, and luckily for his fans, it's something he plans to continue doing for a long time.

"To me songwriting is the backbone of Nashville," said Jackson. "Looks can go, fads can go, but a good song lasts forever."

His string of top-charting albums goes on.

In 1999, he released *Under the Influence,* followed by *When Somebody Loves You* in 2000. In 2002 he released two albums, *Drive* and *Let It Be Christmas. Greatest Hits Volume II* came out in 2003, featuring CMA's Musical Event of the Year, "It's Five O'Clock Somewhere," a single that Jackson performs with Jimmy Buffett. In 2004 he released *The Very Best of Alan Jackson,* along with *What I Do,* which reached the top of the pop and country charts within one week of its release. In

> *Jackson loves performing, but songwriting is closest to his heart, and he plans to continue doing it for a long time.*

Jackson accepts his award at the first ever Country Music Television Flameworthy Awards Show in 2002. Since 1990, Jackson has been a fixture at all the major country music awards shows.

early 2006, Jackson's gospel album *Precious Memories* went on sale. He had recorded the album, which features Denise and two of their daughters, as a Christmas gift for his mother and mother-in-law.

Since 1990, Alan Jackson has been a fixture at the Country Music Association Awards, the Academy of Country Music Awards, and the TNN Music City Awards. He's been honored many times, winning more than 50 top awards, including Music Video of the Year, Album of the

Year, Single of the Year, Song of the Year, Entertainer of the Year, and Male Vocalist of the Year. Many of these honors were given to him more than once.

But Jackson feels most honored when he's able to help those in need. Over the years, he's helped many special organizations, such as St. Jude's Children's Research Hospital and the Down Syndrome Association of Middle Tennessee. One of the Jacksons' very favorite charities is Angel's House, an emergency shelter for the children of his hometown, Newnan, and Coweta County.

Jackson feels most honored when he helps those in need. Over the years, he's helped many special organizations.

The Jacksons even named the house. A statement read during the dedication said, "Our prayer for each child is that heavenly and earthly angels will surround them and protect them at this facility and they will feel truly safe and secure."

Following the devastating effects of hurricanes Katrina and Rita in 2005, Jackson took part in "The Country Reaches Out: An Opry Benefit for the American Red Cross." He also donated autographed jeans to a fundraising auction.

Meanwhile, Jackson's popularity seems to be growing as big as his heart. Country Music Television hailed Alan Jackson as one of the "Greatest Men of 2005." He was also nominated as the 2005 Entertainer of the Year and Male Vocalist of the Year at the Country Music Association Awards.

Alan Jackson poses with his mother, Ruth (far left), and Mattie , Denise, Dani, and Alexandra at the 2004 dedication ceremony for the Alan Jackson Highway in Newnan, Georgia.

Jackson continues to tour and enjoys performing with other entertainers, including Martina McBride, Lee Ann Womack, and the Wrights. The Wrights are a singing duo that just happens to consist of Jackson's nephew Adam Wright and Adam's wife, Shannon.

Jackson maintains that if all his fame disappears tomorrow, well that's okay, too. Good values, family, and friends — these are the things that really matter to him. Believe it or not, if the glare of being a country music superstar fades, it's no problem. Jackson says he'll just whistle for his dog, pick up a fishing pole, and throw in a line.

CHRONOLOGY

1958	Alan Eugene Jackson is born on October 17 in Newnan, Georgia
1979	Alan and Denise get married
1985	Denise meets Glen Campbell in an airport and gives him Alan's demo tape; the Jacksons move to Nashville, Tennessee
1989	Jackson is the first artist to sign a recording deal with Arista Records Country Division
1990	*Here in the Real World* is released; Jackson wins an Academy of Country Music Award for Top New Male Vocalist; daughter Mattie Denise is born
1992	Jackson wins a Country Music Association Award for Music Video of the Year for "Midnight in Montgomery"
1993	Daughter Alexandra Jane is born
1995	The Country Music Association names Jackson Entertainer of the Year
1997	Daughter Dani Grace is born
2002	The Country Music Association honors Jackson with five awards, including Entertainer of the Year; he wins his first Grammy, for Best Country Song, for "Where Were You (When the World Stopped Turning)"
2003	He wins the Country Music Association's Entertainer of the Year title for the third year in a row; "It's Five O'Clock Somewhere," which he sings with Jimmy Buffett, stays at number one on the country charts for eight weeks
2004	Jackson hits no. 1 with "Remember When" and tours with Martina McBride
2005	After Hurricanes Katrina and Rita pound the Gulf Coast, Jackson performs in "The Country Reaches Out: An Opry Benefit for the American Red Cross"
2006	Releases gospel album *Precious Memories*

DISCOGRAPHY

Albums

2006	*Precious Memories*
2004	*The Very Best of Alan Jackson*
	What I Do
2002	*Drive*
	Let It Be Christmas
2000	*When Somebody Loves You*
1999	*Under the Influence*
1998	*High Mileage*
1996	*Everything I Love*
1995	*Greatest Hits Collection*
1994	*Who I Am*
1993	*Honky Tonk Christmas*
1992	*A Lot About Livin' (And a Little 'Bout Love)*
1991	*Don't Rock the Jukebox*
1990	*Here in the Real World*

Singles

2004 "Remember When"

2003 "It's Five O'Clock Somewhere" (with Jimmy Buffett)

2002 "Drive (For Daddy Gene)"

2001 "Where Were You (When the World Stopped Turning)"

2000 "Murder on Music Row" (with George Strait)
"Where I Come From"
"www.memory"

1998 "Right on the Money"

1996 "Everything I Love"
"Little Bitty"

1995 "Tall, Tall Trees"

1994 "Gone Country"
"Hole in the Wall"
"I Don't Even Know Your Name"

1994 "Let's Get Back to Me and You"
"Livin' on Love"
"Thank God for the Radio"
"Who I Am"

1993 "Chattahoochee"

1992 "She's Got the Rhythm (And I Got the Blues)"

1991 "Don't Rock the Jukebox"
"Midnight in Montgomery"
"Pop a Top"

1990 "Chasin' That Neon Rainbow"
"Here in the Real World"
"I'd Love You All Over Again"
"Wanted"

FURTHER READING

For Young Adults

Nash, Alana. "Alan Jackson." *USA Weekend*. November 3, 2002.

Pace-Longino, Miriam. "Alan Keeps Feet Planted in Real World." *Atlanta-Journal Constitution*. September 9, 2001.

Schardi, Kati. "Singer of Simple Songs Connects in a Big Way." *Tallahassee Democrat*, November 7, 2003, p. D22.

Works Consulted

Nash, Alana. *USA Weekend*, "Alan Jackson," November 3, 2002.

Pace-Longino, Miriam. *Atlanta Journal-Constitution*. "Alan Keeps Feet Planted in Real World." September 9, 2001.

Schardi, Kati. *Tallahassee Democrat*, "Singer of Simple Songs Connects in a Big Way," November 7, 2003.

CMA Awards Database, Artist Detail: "Alan Jackson" http://www.cma awards.com/2005/database/ArtistDetail.aspx?artistId=28

"Alan Jackson Doesn't Need a Mansion," January 30, 2006, http://www.gactv.com/news/GACnews/GACnews-update.html

On the Internet

Alan Jackson.com: The Official Website of Alan Jackson.

http://www.alanjackson.com/home/

Angel's House Website

http://www.theangelshouse.org/index.html

CMT.com

http://www.cmt.com/

Rock on the Net: Alan Jackson

http://www.rockonthenet.com/artists

INDEX